ORIGINS OF THE SYMA SPECIES

ORIGINS OF THE SYMA SPECIES

Tares Oburumu

Foreword by Kwame Dawes

University of Nebraska Press / Lincoln

Acknowledgments for the use of copyrighted material appear on
pages 51–52, which constitute an extension of the copyright page.

The University of Nebraska Press is part of a land-grant
institution with campuses and programs on the past, present, and
future homelands of the Pawnee, Ponca, Otoe-Missouria, Omaha,
Dakota, Lakota, Kaw, Cheyenne, and Arapaho Peoples, as well as
those of the relocated Ho-Chunk, Sac and Fox, and Iowa Peoples.

∞

The African Poetry Book Series is operated by the African
Poetry Book Fund. The APBF was established in 2012 with
initial support from philanthropists Laura and Robert
F. X. Sillerman. The founding director of the African
Poetry Book Fund is Kwame Dawes, Holmes University
Professor and Glenna Luschei Editor of *Prairie Schooner*.

Library of Congress Cataloging-in-Publication Data
Names: Oburumu, Tares, author. | Dawes, Kwame
Senu Neville, 1962– writer of foreword.
Title: Origins of the Syma species / Tares
Oburumu ; foreword by Kwame Dawes.
Description: Lincoln : University of Nebraska Press,
2024. | Series: African poetry book series
Identifiers: LCCN 2023039696
ISBN 9781496237026 (paperback)
ISBN 9781496239129 (epub)
ISBN 9781496239136 (pdf)
Subjects: BISAC: POETRY / African | LCGFT: Poetry.
Classification: LCC PR9387.9.Y46 O75 2024
DDC 821/.92—dc23/eng/20231004
LC record available at https://lccn.loc.gov/2023039696

Set in Garamond Premier.

For Tubor

CONTENTS

FOREWORD

KWAME DAWES

In his poem "The Origin," Tares Oburumu's capacity for the arresting line is starkly demonstrated: "At the end of my happiness is a house without doors." There is something quite memorable about this locution, and it is rich with feeling and clever with its own wit and sophistication. Of course, it helps that it makes sense in the way that the best poetic lines should—in layers and layers of meaning that are enlivened and complicated by what a reader might bring to the idea. But for each of these moments of elegant revelation, there are those of unsettling density created, perhaps, by Oburumu's loyalty to the lyric modernist who dances between the received myths of tradition and literary practice (the shared, one supposes, myths), and the private myths of Oburumu—those that may be explained by their use and repetition or that may remain tantalizingly obscure.

This combination is what makes *Origins of the Syma Species* an alluring work of verse emerging from the imagination of a poet who has been formed by our current global spaces of overwhelming access to information—an unmitigated availability that at once contracts the world and its meanings and yet, at the same time, explodes the very meaning of meaning. The African poet working today is caught in this enriched space of possibility and bewilderment. Oburumu is exactly such a poet, ranging the world with gleeful freedom, often crossing borders without care for the niceties of customs offices, passports, and visas; his poems are not postcards home but dispatches celebrating movement and willful appropriations.

In his poems Oburumu is as much fascinated by the world around him as he is with the place of poetry. African poetry is touched by a theoretical reflection that troubles the challenge of a postcolonial poetic—one marked by the hard realities of a colonial education and the emotional and aesthetic weight of Western imperialism. Oburumu allows for his own vulnerability by implicating himself:

Modern African poetry floats irregularly
on water.
On Shaban. Today's Shaban.
It doesn't drown on dates,
nor lean on anything else but Alice & I,
leaving Batham River,   sailing
through drought, music or specter, to euphony;
the afterworld,   looking for some River Thames
shining as oil on sundial;
a lighthouse
seen from the Mediterranean blue, tired of its Hispanic lure.

All my life I have been an English child.
I speak my Arabic like I have a golden tooth.
Careful less I break the languages into more particles.
    ("The Eulogy & a Brief Description of Buckingham House")

In "Surrogacy" Oburumu presents, through a series of intentionally elusive allusions, a kind of poetic autobiography, a poem that dances around the influences, and this dance is both playful and earnest. One imagines that in the first line, he has invented a poet called Amy Lorde, probably and temptingly a conglomerate figure mashing Audre Lorde with Amy Lowell. Lorde seems to make obvious sense, but Lowell, if this is a correct read, is a clever and important figure—one of the great early American poets of the twentieth century.

Amy Lorde was the first poet—living lonely—in verses,

to love me down from poem to poem—even
to the last sonneteer.

She is the genius loci who taught me how to live
with substitution using flowers & presages.
    I was young like a seedling,

always diagonal to life, sunlight & learning.

Geographical too, seasonal, always
two borders away from suicide;
   the not-too-bright world the sunny side of Sylvia Plath.

At the end of the movement the shadowy mood and unsettling angst of
Sylvia Plath arrives, though Oburumu finds himself "two borders away from
suicide"—where the borders are also of geography, race, and gender. These
are all clever ways for Oburumu to lay out his troubled anxieties of influence,
even as the poem effectively pays homage to these voices. There are, of course,
others in "surrogacy," for Oburumu considers himself something of a surrogate,
too, an offspring who is quite skeptical about his own paternity.

Yet Oburumu finds a different and more familial legacy closer to him. In a
beautiful poem that tells the story of a man (his father) and his children trav-
eling on a canoe toward the sea, whether going fishing or escaping one place
for another, or merely enjoying the possibilities of travel, Oburumu is really
interested in the grand symbol, the mythic construction of elemental features
of the making of this artist. The father is a painter, perhaps a painter of myths,
of the imagination, and then there is the "grand sister" who has passed. There
are these oracular figures in Oburumu's cosmology, tied to the environment
and tied to his complex sense of spiritual and mythic understanding:

He keeps painting, silent to the years gone, dreaming, *If she had been with
us, Ebra, your grand sister. If she had stayed a little longer, the sea would have
been more beautiful tonight, Tares. Don't you think she's our star?* he asks,
the net's edge cutting freely the lines across my palm by which, when she's

oracular, she could tell what empty day it is, or if we are predestined for the cuttlefish to come with ease & nightly. I grope to catch my father's voice with what is left of my ears to sift. His cold prayer, which barely survived her death, calls home, which tells me to light a lamp. I know what he means when his lips droop the words on her last breath: *Tell the child to forgive us for these lamps when he's grown, what we meant was a lantern over a paper golden on desk, the pen his paddle, this boat his room.* Take my hands for yours, he says finally, haul over the net to where I can't touch your oar, row. The night is endless, so is every rose; the lamp that will lead you out of the sea, always out of reach.

    ("Let There Be Lamplight")

Oburumu is torn between this sense of Africa and the Englishness of his poetics and his idea of what is poetry and art. It is not a mere replay of the Walcottian dilemma—the love, as it were of the English tongue—but something more cynical and despairing. Of course, in the end, this Sussex, this English is complicated, broken and unsettling. Near the end of the collection a peculiar statement demands a tonal test—is it irony, resignation, dark humor, or a combination of the lot, when he writes, ". . . of the Lord who comes / in the name of a poet"?

    & take Sussex for the Sahara, summer for the harmattan. The people or the poetry of Sussex, when you, by verse, deserve to make honey for it, they wax blacker. I do not, for the type of British education received from Fenie, blackball the love. I have ripe bees in my fingers. My keypads come pollinated. Though I pretend Black as my fingers visualize the origin of night, my body is English, my mind English, my soul made in English. If God wasn't an Englishman, my spirit, where would you be eternal? Perhaps in the little town of Bane, built by water. You are a fish hunter, not a historian as all writers are.

    ("Maud, or Letter to the White Egrets")

There is no question that this is a deeply felt dilemma that generates questions for which Oburumu has no clear answers. "If God wasn't an Englishman, my spirit, where would you be eternal?" he asks. The "Englishness" of "God" happens to be a poetic question, as well, a question of craft, of influence, and of social and creative identity. Without needing to state it explicitly, Oburumu seems fully aware that this condition of messiness is a mark of a certain kind of Africanness—a enactment of what is often inadequately called African cosmopolitanism.

Of course, in this poem the white egret is an artful homage to Derek Walcott and his dilemma from "A Far Cry from Africa," in which Walcott asks the question that, in one incarnation of the self, haunts him for his whole career: "how choose / Between this Africa and the English tongue I love?"

Another less angst-ridden figure will emerge in later Walcott, and one that I suspect appeals to Oburumu—that of the Shabine figure from "Schooner Flight," who returns in different forms in *Omeros*. This figure would seem to have made a choice for a new Caribbean or postcolonial identity—whole and complex but hardly divided. In the wonderful wrestling with this is something extremely beautiful and meaningful. Note how Oburumu's poem turns lyric when he alludes to Walcott—the manner, especially, in which he invokes the sea as a mythic space of disquiet and possibility. Yet Oburumu remains fully ground in his own landscape and in his own peculiar desperation about the limitations of language, the limitations, if you will, of poetry:

Fishing is an art we compare liberally to religion, literature & philosophy. We study donors only.

At the confluence, I offer you the logic of the blue albatross circling above that depth for what it has found. Then the white egrets swift to their vow to keep us fruitful to the end of the sea come along. To the place-names where water is erased for the brown herons to stand as hope among a hem of dead reeds. Row, I cry, seeing the rosary clasped against the paddle lightening your grip go increasingly Catholic, counting the miles even though we have not been Christians but two southern lovers since God spoke our portion of earth into church & politburo; rowing, this gift, is our only way to reach the birds.

("Maud, or Letter to the White Egrets")

The birds, of course, are the destination, but the path to the birds involves a discarding of certain imported faiths ("earth into church & politburo"). Oburumu takes hold of three Walcottian birds, the white egret, the swift, and the heron, all of them representing what he calls "hope among a hem of dead." In this, then, we find Oburumu delight in this art and his resignation to its necessity in his life, a force that has vowed "to keep us fruitful to the end of the sea." At the end of "Maud, or Letter to the White Egrets," Oburumu finds them standing "on the precipice of a world different from the white egrets', calling out for Maud's holy hands screaming, *Touch me, poetry*." It is unabashedly melodramatic and equally desperate to acknowledge Oburumu's urgent need for poetry. Yes, Oburumu borrows Walcott's Maud, the wife of Major Plunket in the epic poem *Omeros*, but what is striking is that Maud, like the classics, simply cannot console enough.

These intimate empathetic connections with certain major women poets, such as Anne Sexton, Yvonne Vera, and Sylvia Plath, offer Oburumu curious points of affinity around the tragic idea of the suicidal genius, yet these leaps of fantasy are his own troubled reflections of gender. In "Music, or Immortality" Oburumu returns to the self—troubled, alone, and finding some possibility in the art of the imagination:

She wore me well, this broken heart could still dream & be dreamt of.
Elsewhere, as I have heard, women make those who wear them well immortal.
Vera Phils became that immortality, perhaps for the night.
I went home with all my shadows trailing, as I do not do every other night, mended.

Origins of the Syma Species is a truly exhilarating debut collection by a poet who has allowed himself to take great risks of form and subject, and one is loath to even suggest any kind of tempering of these poetic excursions, even when they wobble elegantly. Tares Oburumu is certainly a poet with a head full of ideas, but he also has the skill as a craftsperson and the emotional vocabulary and capacity to create poems of power, freshness, and urgency.

ORIGINS OF THE SYMA SPECIES

BOOK 1

Emerging

The night enters my solitude through the Romani clock
on my wall;
a warm circle of lamp gives light to the thousand words
before me,
the great Langstons, poetic not political, on a desk.

The window opens a new river,
a still bed accentuates the meaning of sleep at the far end.
Childhood & towboats reveal the art of a wall gecko
using the silhouettes as its trap.
A moth flies in semicircles, afraid of the dark.
The holy shelf wants a touch, a simple church; a worship.

My mind like fingers flips through the people,
their historical facts, wars, the geography of love.
I give all the glory to the first book I read at the age of 5
my very first entry into lighteners.
Glory to you, aurora, still open to me, colorful like photo albums,
at 32.
Legendary is its broken spine, covered yet in gold dust,
that never closes, never opens, though like Saint Gertrude's hands
clasped in prayer, it is the most blessed image of my father's past,
the horizontal purple in its oaken shelf

sharing love & history, light & darkness with Achebe's *Things Fall Apart*,
now a glasshouse.
This building as Christine, Biafra's mistress,
repainted it with defunct phrases

in her love letter to a child that died, after they divided the country
with handsaws
into two rivers, was once a room they brought by picture
to a land heaving to bridge the gap between what was, what keeps coming
as if there is no end to the grand work on nation building or progress.
As if heaven was not built by man.

After the fall of the sun-stained windows, a door unhinged its bolted grief
to let a boy crawl out of loss, to what would not define the living.
Above him floats, like a boat off sail, what was imagined; the disruption
of a postcolonial page.
In him now is another house, one they are building without brick, iron,
or glass.

One book-layer, not quite angry,
quite satisfied not with an unread culture of nettles
growing from split ground,
steps heavy on the tendrils & the question mark
seen at the end of survival sags
sinks beneath me standing footless beside an infertile block
or word asking not to know where to plant the sun.

Asking to know when we should all fall down on love
with our knees & restart the biblical work of Eden.
Playing from a street piano the notes of my coming out
my father's portion of garden seems not a good place
to neither be bright nor be beautiful,
neither be flower nor tares.

Acts of a Green House

In memoriam. Priest M. Francis.

ACTS 1:1
Prayer & homecoming

"Take my hand, heavenly father,
dip my lips into my own little paradise,
my own little music;
one I have become tender with,
as with the sparrows migrating south.
Let us now ride home with a green heart as headlight
in the shape of a harp,
let us now ride home on a sweet nostalgia,
shape of a godly migration.

For I have surrendered to you
my Volkswagen,
I have surrendered to you
my bugs."

ACTS 1:2
Translating Maud

& everything that has ever been played
with an amber guitar
shining bright under the sun,
                              or under capitalism;
the least of Maud Martha's last prayers
for her practiced body
dispersed toward the common Hague.
                    She's part of the listening,

at peace with the anxious moment,
told to write letters to a country I do not belong to,
though it forces me by law & love to belong to it.
She writes from her world-lit cubicle an eulogy
to the parishioners
who are to donate to every economy a good holy Ghost.

ACTS 1:3
Jesus wept, shortly, for the rise & fall of poetry

back in the havening, clustered & tense
the churches, as big as the country, keep expanding
among the cobblers & the taxi drivers,

                                            where I am but a small poet of
a small calling; Sarojini Naidu
who caches words in her small pockets.
In whose closed hands there's nothing
as crisp as the word martyr,
                        just stanzas of some intricate lines shaking off dust.
Most Sundays, if indoors is not lucky enough,
I let the choir take my voice,
lustra: five heavens deep in the same dream,
the visions chrism-wet
          separate me into the damned more millennial
than the fate of angels vocally adrift,
alto-bright but off-tone.

ACTS 1:4
An ode, not to betrayal

Among the people from nowhere,
I am the only one from Lagos
                  close to myself
standing by a modern piano

digital in its white & black magnificence;
the pedals being everything one can sacrifice a full life
or a little death for:
Take my hand & give its map back to me,
O precious Lord.
Take my lips & my fingers,
O precious Lord.
Lead me not into the goodbye waters,
man at the liquid borders,
O baptismal flight . . .

The music consists of a man
becoming the Old & the New Testaments
& Judas Iscariot kissing Helen on her fingers
yellow with Gethsemane
as tender as fruits ripening.

ACTS 1:5
How to not be, first, as a Nigerian.

There is war also at Lekki
stained with flags & blood as the music is,
                        the guns go ubiquitous,
they are trigger sweet.
The notes buffer, like grasshoppers hooked on milkweed
the wind excites.

ACTS 1:6
To the church made of glass

What girl should know the stones named after a harlot,
what bullfrog is Mary's hypocrisy?
We have pipers who couldn't have been made Vatican,
had God been less political in speaking his native tongue.

ACTS 1:7
Annie Kay's miracle & the school of average

Do you know you can say anything
& everything comes all at once?
Say "let us be light" then there will be Thomas
feeding the multitude with doubt,
throwing the leftovers in green baskets
at the congregation shouted down.
                                        A sea appears above the altar,
where the new converts can walk by their boats to the beach
holding a party for William's daughter
in whom is the malpractice, the shining stun,
a multiplication of scores by sex, hierarchically.
I take her by no foot of hers to the eastern mountain
& show her the kingdom of God, the light of sin.

ACTS 1:8
Book of politics, book of hunger

Under this universe the city is a far-flung darkness
over tumblebugs, farads, dead flags & a grace dying in her hands.
This is the height she aspires to, same pinnacle
so much done for, an acme which aspires to her.
6,000 feet above sea level, the reach, like God,
growing higher & higher, she jumps shoulder-down the spire,
with no angel to hold on to,
falling in response to whatever language I must have breathed
to mean legacy.
    I do not know how to save you from this fall,
this world, or the next country?
Do not tell, you preach, falling.
Poetry sings the questions, bridges the answers.

Tunnel

What if there is no light at the end,
will Sasha still call it a tunnel, or passage?
That is the north we are indebted to
the moon in the dream we have been looking for.
We, dying in little lives here in William's Town
in a remote island, almost a house with lights turned off,
have not been taught enough how to be dark in the light
& light in the dark, or face the sun
with all our reading lamps.

Along the blue terraces of the Batham River,
you could see the swimmers, water-light, parsing oil vessels.

The happy swans go down into the deep,
the kingfisher, phosphorus, nods approval.
One natural light, by staying with them,
keeps burning out the lamps at sea.
The other surprised by gas flaring butterflies,
not too bright for a future expressed as hourglass
(neither hope nor a sybarite's delight) brings the sun
& its sands down to the night.
I thought, being black as a bastille lacking windows,
I'd seen you, once, blue in Sirius.
Twice have I mistaken you for who I was,
an explorer & believer excessive in the color white—*part of the dark.*

Understand why I dive into an endless ship, wrecked,
lying at the bottom of my soul,

always blue by my keel.
Why I dive into the waves, dreams first before the head.
Then this fate I have been given;
is a chance to find your own light.

Parental Guidance for August Children
Watching the Movie *A Beautiful Mind*

She presses down with a certain adult forte
the bluest button in her hands
& here comes Nash,
a walking gaillardia fresh from the applause,
filling everything in the room: geckos, cobwebs,
hanging cups of light, corrugated doorknobs,
switch boxes, memories in framed family colors,
pockets of walls for bugs or a thousand ants,
various heirlooms, paperwork, the grand odalisque;
this could be the wife looking back at the night & the past,
opposite the solitary window asterisked, perhaps,
by too much leaning on thoughts, head propped
against transparent glass, he wins schizophrenia
& the economy all at once.
Star works overcome my daughter's heartbeat,
exulting the scream: I want my delusion, her cry.
How do I put off the light from Vincent's fame
on same subject, wondering how I could live the question
to the end, as did Alicia, till Stockholm rained the more artistic lights,
the fireflies bred from Princeton.
This place I come from is little less African,
far from sapience, or the sense of duty.
I have been sitting here in this chair
long before she became a child born outdoors
a few days close to August.
My face tuning the TV, honing decades,
waiting for the consequences that come with reading a book
just to fall in love with you, Sasha.

Now I forget to remember the times, most parentally,
on Monday mornings, how I watch, my spine on the stem
overlooking the blackboard on which is the controversy,
What's a miracle?
Voila child! I am the magic down under the window,
the noise more mathematical than a hundred decibels,
drowned the whole numbers.
Your mother rose from her silence & beauty like a brown argus
from a wind-broken hibiscus to terrify the loud work to a stop.
Class resumed its effect more on her
than the years I examined deeply her heraldic innocence
to be the disease I named after the gift of loneliness in a nest of books.
Each door I opened was a door to a number written on another door;
a window to my cure, from which your mother's eyes glistened,
tear-bright, unable to tell from the pictures of the redeemer & the Virgin Mary
hanging above my hair, what could be hospital
& a society of wild geese populating the stream, artificial, at the left side
of the window, chasing fruits thrown at the birds by the inmates
who loved things feathered to the brim.
You could tell, after I met you in a cold afternoon
thinking you are invisible,
from the way I was startled by your pink dress.
I touched the woman in you,
that I do not live in a movie.
But sit here on the history of my laps.
Watch me hope you didn't see me in the pictures.
I live to die by words alone.

My Father's Last Hope for Water

Oil could be the reason I was born in July,
the detritus's best blessing;
between the fishermen & their empty nets,
right off the islanding sands.
A homing boat calls for a lost roost
like a lone seagull.
My father & our fathers' landing,
with the mist haloing, echoes the iambic cry.
I have not read about the *howl* by Allen
Ginsberg,
the egrets' elegies coming through,
one can be sure the old & the new Americans
are not different from us, the living nights.
I hear the declaration, the rustle
the national choir often sings,
rooted on equal shore.
There is a pianist that understands how the river flows
this rainy season.
How the panther understands Black music.
He is slow, troubled & practiced,
lifting his fingers off the white keys when the need
to be Black becomes too important
to ignore his origins.
My father is the origin of all violins,
his elbow's deep roots in the instrument,
find in his imagined delirium
the boat now heading north with debris-light
swollen in its belly

& grandfathers broken all on swamp.
We have been performing funerals all along
fishing in the Ekole River.
I sit as a child on the beach,
my back against the south where I come from.
He gives up the net & the hook,
six fishless years rise with him
as he lifts his sunburned feet to walk on waterweed
across the little brook between us.
His woman, my mother, has been waiting for him
at the end of her life.
Instead of swimming,
he ships his bones over his own liquid shadows,
black in one of the habits which serves him like water,
shapeless.

Illustrations Showing Figures of Speech Left on a Telephone Line Years after the Civil War

For July 6, 1967

To those who evaded the green art of dying,
those who loped
over the eastern hills to live chronicle,
living the sunlight,
condolences.
                You are beautiful just the way
you are,
warhorse panicked by sirens & headlights.

Light is here again, life. The van, an extraordinaire,
shall breathe down the surviving years,
              but I, the more stronger will,
shall take Nicole Sealey with me:
the first person to live a hundred & fifty years has already been born,

as poet & bird, bibliolater.
The maniac I'd wanted to be eludes me.

The war describes the dead as national guard,
still it is the flag, still the sun is alive.

From the balcony on the Niger,
it is 218 BC, you see Hannibal, almost as famous as Sisyphus,
crossing the Alps with an army of eighteen thousand wars.
              The river, sailing as I am over archive & rising yellow,
bears these shapes, salts our history, so it becomes impossible
                      for the red-earth States to decompose.

Yet the babies corrupt by electrolysis, they are water.
Don't you cry, Sasha. I should be the Argentine to shed the rains.
                              The pictures you see today are the colors
painting definite the dreams you have been named after:
Madonna, blue guitar, microphone, nightshade,
a transparent house by crystal sea

                                        standing on a cliff of rock sand.
You hear the bellflowers grow from it,
even as the grenades you thought were pomes ripen in your hands,
then explode.   You know the future
by how durable it is in ruins.
How long you can walk on water in your own shape.
I have asked you, with every book I have read,
to be un-nameable.

                              Things we name
are incomprehensible. Like God. Like Biafra.
Open your mouth,
let the sound ring in its own symbol.
Do I blaspheme what terrifies you?
The Igbos are extraterritorial because we are not of a simple blood.
The generic call for surrender must be love,
                              if life is not a bridge across
                                        a field of roses.
& until the sentimental flowers learn the linear ways to reach the sun,
don't you burn at the capital split.

                        By map & Maya, these boundaries have been my tears,
the milk in a silver cup the baby fathers won't let go.
How I have fallen facedown at the borders.
Father! let this mug pass away from me: nevertheless, not as I will,
but as I drink, praying.

Teaching Metaphysics, or Disciplinal Notes on Self-Culture

For Margaret Fuller (of the New York Herald Tribune*)*

In 1996 I drove in the car I have not forgotten.
Violet, but not enough,
crossing Third Mainland Bridge to the interior mind
from my house made of ghettoes,
call them the poetic rooms,
down St. Voltron to a lake they call oxblood,
translated from the dead living by the waters,
because it was my first day out in a circumference,
                between bright, unbright & leaden,
in my pink shirt the illustrious friends, like lit bulbs,
affected how enlightened I was.
I sat among what terrified as if bombs were about to detonate me;
                my armpit smelled of the only care I'd given it:
                unkempt poetry, Black American music, empty cigarettes.

This life is not mine, it is my mother's & I am God's lifeboat
floated from July weeks before a spendthrift died from wineglass.
In the delta, around the year the beetles chose to make love to the palm trees,
                he thought it was quite safer to die at the time Christ turned water
into the good old drunks,
as it is recorded in a subtext as read with telescopes
than to see the ants in their storehouse.
                            It wasn't a fable the rainy season, it was spiritual.
Standing up to my exit morphed into flesh
from what was invisible, all around me were the jeering lakers
grateful to the women for some darling debts.
                        I know I didn't come to this earth by dust alone.
            Someone must have brought me here by hand?

The Eulogy & a Brief Description of Buckingham House

Modern African poetry floats irregularly
on water.
On Shaban. Today's Shaban.
It doesn't drown on dates,
nor lean on anything else but Alice & I,
leaving Batham River,   sailing
through drought, music or specter, to euphony;
the afterworld,   looking for some River Thames
shining as oil on sundial;
a lighthouse
seen from the Mediterranean blue, tired of its Hispanic lure.

All my life I have been an English child.
I speak my Arabic like I have a golden tooth.
Careful less I break the languages into more particles.
Mother & child arrive at miscegenation   (in 2002)
the beautiful Buckingham,
the biography of John Nash, only the white girls can read;
architectural prose written by a lover & her two sphinxes.
                    Indoors is an invisible labyrinth.
It is hard for me to tell
which of our shadows is glass or wood
when the angels finally open the city walls
to the Flaming June.   Here, anything can be your dream
if you practice fortune.   Pray fantasists to sleep, or go fluid &
reversible, winning the rose
with the cold of eight winters in your hands.

Surrogacy

Amy Lorde was the first poet—living lonely—in verses,

to love me down from poem to poem—even
to the last sonneteer.

She is the genius loci who taught me how to live
with substitution using flowers & presages.
                            I was young like a seedling,

always diagonal to life, sunlight & learning.

Geographical too, seasonal, always
two borders away from suicide;
                  the not-too-bright world the sunny side of Sylvia Plath.

This is the doom which comes from your gift
   —the schoolyard hunting you down
to the end of the
alphabets.

I remember how someone kept burning
                         the lamplight
for her poetry
                Emmett Till's mistletoe
still shining from the dark,
because people are noisy lights,
silence becomes a genre of art.

How she kept blowing out the last breath
                              scrambled for.

Lazarus Baby, would you have survived an American
if they had exchanged your starburst for mine?
Before you ducked, did you ever see my country
pieced with the mystery I am,
running past the noose each time the sky is let down from a tree?
I am what I am,
the afterimage, the deathwatch dying.
Do I terrify my own terror?
I remember how lovely you would have been,
if you had seen your diamond your other self
read the amphitheater into a galaxy,
God on your feet,
invulnerable to the childhood you had in a vacuum.

Heaven is for those who are liable to
                              but will not die this young,
says my elegy,

wading through slough & prayers to a backwater
which is home, a discontinuance.

My gaze goes multidimensional regarding the sea,
                  its blue horizon on which I was raised a cipher
living the ocean.

To every egret, a cry is given. To every shore, a grave
that won't be quiet.
                  To everyday, is a requiem. It writes roughly the waters

on which the happier boats, carrying light of the Natives,
row to nowhere near fulfillment, imperial in a contrived

isolation or island.

Water raised me.
                    What fish could have done better than us?
The white egrets,
imagine the splendor in their feathered eyes,
                              imagine the blue sails
as we the greater salmon
swam through to our breakfast of beef
canned in floating boxes the boats threw at us.

I wanted to know how deep is their love for a seaman.
I climbed up, a boy close to the cabin where curiosity animates.
Here, through the keyholes, it animates the misery index.
On a cardboard paper were names dug with colors
we were not taught in school by an uncle not an ordinary chef.
A cabin boy I could charge with a lunchbox.
Is this the love he asked of his internment, or lovelorn voyage?
He was the door. He wore the door as a young boy's Christmas dress.
He wore it on the gown; the mark of his six years reading to death
an economy depressed at the brain, a branch
of collegiate flame.
He was the name Talbot John they supplanted with Jacob,
on the list he read himself as a man becoming.
He was burning at the nights he rose from his dreams
about the ladies he could have loved.
Each for a beauty practiced in the streets.
He was the flame & what gave it light.
Love is a sledgehammer in the hand of the one who wields it.
It is heavy where it is lightweight, weightless where it is heavy.
I could count on my fist dipped in sand, not the fist,
those who have lost a head or two
loving what they cannot love: a country,
a girl who dangles her beauty in her hands like a sword.
I could not wait for the waters to take me home,
alone in myself.

When the school bell rang,
                    I remembered how young I was,
leaf on wave going home to what I believed in.
                              I believed in you, Sira; prime

of the beautiful sexagenarian, my father the art of all hope.

When the waves met me at the riverbank,

                    I remembered

how old I would have been
when the roses open up   their petals to let the surfs
touch their thorns
                    with the blessings of a child.

By liminal sunray, grow.

By water & grace, grow.

          Death is still not the life you are taking.

By word & spiracles, grow.

               Sing the Gloria in Excelsis.

By music & disaster, live.

               Glory be to Sylvia in excelsis.
                         Believe too in the other guitars she plays.

You are to hear the angels sing,

but do not listen.

Let There Be Lamplight

For every tunnel there is a rose growing at the end

It is the night of February 25, 1997, the sea becomes a branch of art again: my father's painting of a tunnel. He does this like a child raised by Vincent van Gogh, when we float between the long island & the forest, almost a corridor, blurred to a solitary heron calling for the white heat the horizon. *We are at the Groundless*, he whispers, to remind me of some familiar fear or water which keeps coming to us in the same vein we keep going to it, rowing to a vow we each must declare to dissever the fragments of a brother I buried here. He is a son couched in no ordinary love, articulated in the volume his lungs can take when he talks fluently about dying. This is the place with no bedrock, just faith & water. Once I have dipped my fingers in it, the sand under the blue waves felt the touch from the hand of a fisherman, twice my father sank a forest of two palm trees into what he calls Endless. They are endless, the fish with no foundations. The mystery six fathoms deep, knowing love drowned here, groks itself. Brisking up to us is the water's quiet promise to keep us salted in the frontline, braving the canoe for what we know must not come. He keeps painting, silent to the years gone, dreaming, *If she had been with us, Ebra, your grand sister. If she had stayed a little longer, the sea would have been more beautiful tonight, Tares. Don't you think she's our star?* he asks, the net's edge cutting freely the lines across my palm by which, when she's oracular, she could tell what empty day it is, or if we are predestined for the cuttlefish to come with ease & nightly. I grope to catch my father's voice with what is left of my ears to sift. His cold prayer, which barely survived her death, calls home, which tells me to light a lamp. I know what he means when his lips droop the words on her last breath: *Tell the child to forgive us for these lamps when he's grown, what we meant was a lantern over a paper golden on a desk, the pen his paddle, this boat his room.* Take my hands for yours, he says finally, haul over the net to where I can't touch your oar, row. The night is endless, so is every rose; the lamp that will lead you out of the sea, always out of reach.

Maud, or Letter to the White Egrets

I

At 4 in a Swazi morning, when I am done studying the sunny asterisks in the night sky, I have no sins. I drink lemonade for prose, fall featherweight on southeastern music & sleep, blue sugar to a few memories revised, anamneses my friends & Tandzile call dreams. I do not emplace mine in eulogies as divine transversals either, I portend nothing, nothing portends me, except this room the size of heaven, where my belief in the universe first took root, like the taproot of the *Tectona grandis*, which grew into a young Bantu; the last son of Maud Martha hours after she died by ruth. What she ever wanted wasn't a dream. She was the dream. She was both night & day; a series of walks down an unknown street with a visual God in her hands, the New Jerusalem; or a New South Africa, the height I have been crossing countries for to plant my ambitions, call them flowers. My lovers, my b-girl among them for whom long-distance journeys start with violins, couldn't wait for the sun to break cloud. Marley's love driving us from the stereo in the mist, we, helping him with our baritone, play the car rather through the green savannah arteries. We come to the zebra at the city gate, not only by sound but by color also, when the leonine need not to be more than horses arises from a land we are part of by being dust as they are. Sometimes in April, as clear as I can never forget, we hit a mare to death while imagining a good veal marengo. Today, the animals repeating themselves, we have to stop the music, stop the wheels completely, to let the human race pass. Eventually, if we wait that long, the town's map will open one sordid door by broken door. When all waiting is done, the future will realize its presence in gold. Welcome to Eden, reads the milestone, then the abundance of advancement, Eve & Adam naked in such realistic innocence we shall rename light, the light the dead thirst for, the florescence we do not see. At last we retire to a hotel from which we could look down at the world a city in separate clusters, the traffic in supernational flights of unknowing. Why don't you come down to naïveté, call the children, more African than their fathers colonial in all understanding? How can they, divided in two by a Briton & a nation, hear what to listen to when the music is full of Native tongues? Ah! violin, violence, after all these Eswatini years, would you still break our father's first symphony?

2

For Dawn Ayanate

& take Sussex for the Sahara, summer for the harmattan. The people or the poetry of Sussex, when you, by verse, deserve to make honey for it, they wax blacker. I do not, for the type of British education received from Fenie, blackball the love. I have ripe bees in my fingers. My keypads come pollinated. Though I pretend Black as my fingers visualize the origin of night, my body is English, my mind English, my soul made in English. If God wasn't an Englishman, my spirit, where would you be eternal? Perhaps in the little town of Bane, built by water. You are a fish hunter, not a historian as all writers are. A descendant of Nimrod, feminine Genesis; manliness is this pearl you wear around your neck. On crossing the river on fiber-love, you a hill at the back, I, a granule on the bow hauling the distal ends between woman & man, between fish & hunger, live deeply to find the depth of us; hunger being an art from which the body becomes God. Behind us flare the gases, the water shining under that desolation can be described as Sylvan, hemmed in by mangrove trees as massive as a leviathan. Fishing is an art we compare liberally to religion, literature & philosophy. We study donors only.

At the confluence, I offer you the logic of the blue albatross circling above that depth for what it has found. Then the white egrets swift to their vow to keep us fruitful to the end of the sea come along. To the place-names where water is erased for the brown herons to stand as hope among a hem of dead reeds. Row, I cry, seeing the rosary clasped against the paddle lightening your grip go increasingly Catholic, counting the miles even though we have not been Christians but two southern lovers since God spoke our portion of earth into church & politburo; rowing, this gift, is our only way to reach the birds. I hold on to the girl you were, breasting the athenaeum, like the turtles of the Songs of Solomon, speed of light under water, singing from flesh to bone, bone to flesh the lines bolstering the boat to what ray of hope there is under the seabirds. The surfs, as high as roofs, roll in the blue chorus for two Maecenases the living brooks. We know the words *we are drowning* to be liquid, at the moment of dying translated as what transcends the lotus the glory of a rose on wave. The water consoles. Already the white egrets have received the letter. We are not sure if they can read what the signature says: *The dead are called "Gone too soon" but all around you is water.* Now I stand on the precipice of a world different from the white egrets', calling out for Maud's holy hands screaming, *Touch me, poetry.*

Paradise

We arrived at the Apapa Wharf, covered with mist.
A piece of sun burning in my hands. & keeping
to my brown shadows heavy in the lives of seafarers,
full of water, I sat beside a heap of stones,
offering the net a comfortable place. Above us
shone the late moon. We shook with dew
& a loveliness strange in a fitting way. While there,
I untangled one fish after another, quiet & happy
home to the knowledge of the Godhead watching over my mother,
the water woman.
Behind us, the village slept, huffing up the night's dream.
We talked silently, into the hours, singing the Noel;
It was Christmas in Quidah, a time for the trees in the prairie,
of bright moments & altos. It was the first time I heard my mother
laugh. It was when the slave ships on her dress broke down,
as she dipped her fingers in the threaded ocean.
I placed the tunas in one basket, raising my voice
to the reach of her joy that we have, finally, found a way to live.

Syma Minor

The war came through the arc of the island. The boat,
stopped by the bullets, drowned. How it went down
in graceful bends. How they jumped on the forest
with their backs wet with escape. She turned her head
to the world, as if asking in small measures, as if afraid
to ask what mercy is made of, why the dead are always
the love we, gorgeously, get to hold in our hands. The child
held her shoulders, heavier than breath in times
of fear, quiet, knowing a sound will wake the graves,
opening, closing as they ran. How the baby soldier,
dressed in innocence, pointed the muzzle at the love
he once missed as a child. The leaves revealed the day,
as he shot the mother on the heart where the colors,
cried from her daughter's depths, made shallow
on the beach, to attract the others hidden under the things
they could not see. Once, in my tours around what
was a literary museum, I brought the girl to a gathering
of warring nations, tried hard to save my biography
in the hands of the baby crawling into the stream, the girl
reading how I died to let her live. Now cinnamon
in the arms of her mother.

How to Love the Boats

Swimming is the only gift we have, the only way to write us
out of shipwreck. & an elegy of the marsh says, talent is a ruin
if it is not fed with hope, blessings & disaster. Here in Syma,
each day, we float on the need not to drown. Elsewhere,
a city stands, philosophical, at the shore watching the lovers
of water founder in what they love. Among those who came
to see loss for what it is, are the pianists of the house of Noah.
They came to build the ark with fiddles & a flutter of outlooks.
I placed my mother above their realm, lifted her head up with my hands,
shaped like octaves & swam in the future she doesn't know.
Hurry not, hurry not, she said, *we too will make it to existence.*
Her voice was soft as water. But with the waves cresting my father's laughter
in the peak of a loud town, I rowed my heart into the things
that will save me: my poetry, my mother's beauty & the boats.

BOOK 2

A Long Walk on Endlessness, the City
of J. K. Anowe, the Decembrist

The landscapes of childhood, the geography of dream,
the word for meaning; the world for a centrist
is one step forward into Kuala Lumpur,   two feet backward
to null   moonlight nightie.   What impresses a child?

I choose Malaysian neurosis;
the photograph you sent on Christmas day.
You on a train living in light, a seemingly homecoming,
had the marks of race on it off station,   going elsewhere
to loneliness   a time for the missing string.   Why suffer the violin,
oh violent song?

It is there in the way you smile in flowers.
Of how long you have been walking with a friend
to get to the roses. The roses are as big as infinitude.
Yours are survival instincts in bloom.

I squint to see you scattered in grains,
head obliquely placed on your window
until I headlined the photo: *Brother, who are you living?*

                    They say you have been mad all your life.
& I understand what they mean.

          You have become a fine writer.

Music, or Immortality

The skit

Poetry is the apple
my uncle eats
after every class
he teaches.

He goes home to his woman
who breeds like the fish.
In brass, the ocean is all salt,
no blue. Get a sea job here,
you die from unemployment.

My uncle breeds like the fish.
His music, like the universe, has
its own end where there is no end.

Even when it stops on the stereophonic
sound system, it starts from the
beginning of water.

All through the five decades of the song,
I was penitential for some future I didn't commit.
My hands felt like faults on Vera Alina's waist;
the girl next door I happened upon in the
dancehall.
Stars fell, glistened on the floor. Bodies orbital,
red skin, green skin, white skin, black seemed
a forbidden color. We were dancing the rainbow,
the beauty dizzied me more, the bottled stars

became too much light I barely saw the god
who has forsaken me.
The moon came down that night, the whole galactic house.
A lady I had known for a chorister in a local church
where I was once a contralto, touched my shoulders
where wings had grown so big.
I feared I would become an angel when they fluttered.
One love broken in the human heart,
sooner than later finds its piece in a flock.
My ex-girl's presence was the sun, a volatile Omni.
But I was grateful to my cross; the grace of our Lord, Jesus.
Heartbreaks are not fragments that walk alone.
They are apoptoses with love for the lonely places.
The empty houses peopled by poets I knew as exceptional lovers
of a world that practiced what they cannot love.
It found love guilty when Sylvia overdosed on America.
It made love a small island when Tiara Phils rowed her own boat,
crossed three rivers to drown her beauty in the Atlantic Ocean.
Did she look good in love? or who does?
I thought I would hear her call me by my elegiac name
when I walked out of my empty days through the crescendos
to the guitars' summit; a place for flight.
Just when I thought I had no feathers, music gave me wings.
Love could be dangerous. But I had the heart of a dancer,
elastic, supple with the color yellow.
A woman difficult to love is not difficult to dance with.
Give space. Watch her spin in the hands of a favorite friend.
She is sexual but not openable. Hold her close, closer than a skin.
Give her breath. Breathe into her bodies. Make her a bird.
Light as cotton. Give your arms, your nests.
You are the home where she comes to roost after flight.
Do not stop the music which is now her body,
even though the dance is over.
That night, music became flesh. I was its bone, moving the words

from blood to spirit, the planets surrounded me.
She wore me well, this broken heart could still dream & be dreamt of.
Elsewhere, as I have heard, women make those who wear them well immortal.
Vera Phils became that immortality, perhaps for the night.
I went home with all my shadows trailing, as I do not do every other night,
    mended.
Bedding dreams, I switched on the radio as a tribute
to a night that became dark the moment the station turned off my soul
to the words in marble, spoken on the walls of the room my uncle once
        slept in as a boy
dreamy in the same heirloom I became more sexier than he ever was:
For whom would you breed for, my dear younger uncles? for a country
or for a dead economy?
In the way I fell to sleep, hands raised as if in surrender,
it was visible & bright to know I might have chosen country,
the way I labored drowsily to stop the music.

In the Time of the Telephone

This is how I write to you,
to make you beautiful when the earth breaks you,
Sasha:
Let the maps go before you,
turn on the city lights.
Use the glory of God nine hours a day.
Wash the mirrors off your skin.
Polish where you hurt most
till you become the diamond they love to touch.

Sit on the chair opposite self-denial.
Carry the dream as a cross.
Let the boys know you didn't survive the thorns,
you are the thorn.
Let the phone ring.
Let the messages come bloated with verbs.
Let your hello be religious.
Talk about the Virgin Mary, the mother of God.

The girls of exultation & your sister the brown sugar,
are their own theaters.
The traffic watch them for all things bright.
They don't talk about painting,
they are pearls that need no color.
They are electrical, the lights without which
Lagos is all the darkness as it was in the beginning.
I have to speak the language of light,
to see clearly what they create.

How void were the times highlighting the fruits
they ate to be beautiful?
What makes the Black girls here happy, diamonds,
boys, or apples?
There is always something for them to believe in:
the peacock, a house of glass, the camera.
Each carries an allegory as halo brace, the untold picture
under the shining skin.
Your mother in knitting her stories for your dress, Sasha,
broke the spindle file
& I was walking from the rock bottom as puppet
in a factory that invented bureaucracy.
For months, I climbed the stairs for completion.
How I sought needle but found silk instead.
This was how your mother wrote you in patches:
a tablecloth, a thorn & a button.
She could not tell if you looked feminine.
We knew you would become an angel;
days on the phone with him, you keep talking about the dress,
Saint Gertrude's prayers & the boys of Syma, the sea's agnates.
You measured well the ocean between word & deed.
You told him boats do not float on bubbles, they sink.
That you do not want love, you want ambivalence.
Then you kissed him goodbye with the portrait of your saint
pinked on your lips.
Your very best.   *Father,*   *forgive them*
for they do not know how to fall in love, you pray.

Running

Hand in hand on a piano as two dissidents
& lovers, we are making, with slow fingers,
a music for the war-torn alto dead in the little girl
the hourglass made womanly with desert sand
& begin again the work of love.
I wolf through the door, a guardian angel to Mariah,
midnight mother under the arms of a small father,
young enough to believe love can be made on a nest of bullets.
He had his thirst undressed & had begun the work
of creation.
His silent rifle length of his body laid beside the mosquito net
& a lamp burning as witness.
From the battlefield, my father's house is one big continent,
divided by urge, doors & maps.
Each window is a nation wide open.
There, on the shock where I stood, I touched the trigger,
blessing him with a grave the size of his desire.
Then a burst of gunfire, a rush of footfalls, armored tanks
& the love song of J. Alfred Prufrock, playing:
Let us not die then, you & I.

I held you by the torso, jumped out of the small countries.
& even though we knew we were running in a dream,
we didn't stop running.

How to Love a Girl—Austen College Recital for Pablo Neruda's Genius

This is it, Abigail; the bright Chinese red light,
the dream I had 3,000 years ago. We made it.
Repair the broken orchestra, sweet violins
& go beautiful.
In the fashion of colonizers, wonder boy,
winter child is coming home to winter.

Gorgeous Harare opens the gates named after Harley.
A white Ferrari drives through.
How much I love my country.
You listen as I call you by your Arabic name,
flannelette-Oriental, almost
Safia—the book of Michelangelo,
painted with a burst of stars, the future songs
of his genius.
The green flag is still a green leaf in spite of the locusts raising it.
The historical facts in your eyes, the look in Dylan's face
when they offered him the news
on a plate of poetry; the unhistorical waiting.

Everyone waves at the appearance of a diamond, bright or unbright.
It is pronounced ribaldry here.
Where does it begin to hurt, the Nigerian horizon?
Because you are oblivious.
Because you are heavens upon heavens away from it,
never let go of your heart. Here are my gifts: a month
of indoors outing; your Brazilian hairs
dark on the crescents of my ribs, your fingers framing

the notes of my coined pockets—self-portrait as God
in love with a still panther, a box of chocolates
& jewelries at our feet, the talks about oysters & seamstresses.
An endless T V watching us.
How much I love you.
Do I make you a port or a book club?
With the book of glory, the glory of
the emigrating birds in your hands, opened forever & ever,

Life is beautiful, you sing.

& the I Is the Revolution

The train left in July & rolled till August appeared from mists & brown hills; a house which is also a month in the rain, of beautiful water but not enough. I sat, a dream, in the room with no walls just photographs, watching the country as it sped by. I wanted to be a gardener to the people overgrown with grass. *Jesus, do not defile your journey*, said some lovers. I opened a book instead & fell asleep on long sentences. One was a door, the memory or mirror I have to pass through when I am done studying the days I have yet held, as sunflowers, in my hands. When I was a little of angel, a little of foreshadow, building rails with ink & papers. The travelers stopped at the end of a word where the season drowned in a pool of Biafran soldiers waiting for their babies at the gate of heaven. The war was over on arrival but as father & survivor I had to board another taxi to the place where I was born, first as a painter of the damned then the origin of glory. But there was no driver just flags. So I began with love, leading myself into the next choir. Singing the dream with acoustic guitar & two colors. At home, Lekki was just a flag, just a flag shot in the vein. That was how love began in the South. A mother under rain, looking for water to wash the national blood off her baby. I, waves above water, pluck sunflowers for the little girl's dress. The angel who does not know my name. My name is . . . night sky when on earth the candle lights flicker, petal, wing of macaw, exit, the glory of interventions, call me lone butterfly & I am human.

The Origin

At the end of my happiness is a house without doors.
Everything is shut in. The sun, too, stays in its oval yellow,
the grace. Everything, except the light of my eyes
burning from paper. Do I exist? What, in English, is a home
surrounded by words/dreams called, an island or library?
With exit signs & curtains floating on green lights,
the people being open places or love altered gloriously
to give to my mother, the revolution, a country of lemony fields,
of what she doesn't know, perhaps, an ode to flowers.
It could be a future note for the music vast as the sea between me
& my fathers. As she sits on white chairs from across the flag
almost an easel. I could hear her painting the dialysis she suffers from;
the only way to bridge the music the window the reasons why I write about you,
this universe of water where I come from.

Note 1—a Vision of Afghanistan

For Kabeh & Helen from Northern Nigeria,
loving me from ten thousand wars in that everyday country

Morning, says Kabul.
& I become this auricular kiss you want to hear,
the Vietnamese lips, like flowers,
spread from petal to petal green above the mountains.
The woman in a girl's dress, I see the ages trembling in her.
The flag she wears is a fragment of the stories we share.
She climbs down from cuesta to mesa, with a baby on her back,
quiet as the American dream,
singing, *Dostat daaram,*
dostat daaram—I am not leaving
you, dostat daaram.
Put on the war lights. There is this need
to see clearly the babies walking into Grayson's afterlife.
Stephen Sawyer's America is a rocking chair there.
Sit, let us not talk about dying, today?
We can reach the tomb's end. It is beautiful like the ocean's depth.

But where did our heaven go?
We can't reach that too, unless by a gun to the ideas in our heads?
Send this letter to Hafiz, the second coming. Hafiz, is the sweetest phrase
slicing the country in two. You, seated on its altiplano of politics, I,
climbing my decline.
If I do mean Christ when I call for a poet,
what kind of species have I become,
T. S. Eliot's light?
The Natives have come—self-portrait as Sylvia & Akachi:
angels with grenades in their palms
mapping the instruments of music.

Goodbye, perhaps. & then the Hosanna plays, blessed be the government
which comes in the name of Safia.
Let's talk about Sophia, too. Walk, in step with the steps gone,
into the bomb crater, then detonate.
Become light & more of stars than fireworks.
Interpret what the saxophones sing.
God had said from across two eternities, let there be Afghan,
& there is America, with a little angel there,
a little Northern Nigeria here.
& who holds now the light for the babies gone?
Now growing as hibiscus flowers, witnesses, only,
to a new breed of roses open like garden doors,
looking out from the barrel of a sniper rifle,
who?

Note 2—Syma

Phantasy flowers. The purple in Sylvia's jewels. Morass. Open warren.

Halo be to the child farmed for glory.
Here in a house painted by words, art & how we make love grow from tuft,
dying is a color as fertile as a field of green shrubs in the rainy season.
You were not told?
In my father's country, there are many mansions.
I wouldn't have told you this,
if migration isn't another name for paradise.
We are all headed to mystery. But it takes a day or two for poets
& the church to reach it.
Call it the horizon. Dream utopia, a soft landing for lovers.
I know a little about funerals & caskets,
because the books I read
are shaped like the grave.
Open it, she says. I open.
There is a place I always go,
the dead photograph.
It is me & my debts, we are captured in white.
White, holy are the words of the Lord who comes
in the name of a poet.

Me & my fathers have wasted the earth given to us as water.
Wasted the love where I should have been as happy
as a child in its place of innocence.

There are six glories I tone.
Four I have been given as darkness
burning in the light.

The glory of mirrors, before which I often stand
picking the broken glasses in me.
The glory of sleepless nights.
The glory of my life a pen in my own hands.
The glory of saying goodbye when it is not a time to leave you, Sasha.

I have carried my dead body for too long
it is light as hope, the first word
I wrote down on paper.
I stared long at it until I lost my eyes in it.
Keep looking at yourself, she says. I keep to my words.
Here is Tares lying inside a tomb.
Call it a book, open it, she says. I open.
I look forward like God, the future, don't I?
I look like a music player. Sing me on, origin.
There is no better way to live than being your own endless song.
If there was one, I wouldn't have been written like an exit sign.
If there were no poets who sang like God.
There is a child in every man
that always wants you to love it with roses,
toy boats, milk & butterflies.

In Syma, my mother says many things & they come to pass.

Altar

For Michael Philomena & Sasha

The book in your hands, brilliant planet,
is Bandari's map; your heart.
Find where you shine in the dark, the city.
With it, when you are lost in a maze, living
the tunnels,
you shall be the love
the myth you have been looking for,
the leavener for the dust you are not,
the earth you are.
Be gathered in this paradise;
sit, eat of the letters as you would a burger.
There is a door that leads only to you,
open it.
Read the story of the one
who first loved you behind closed windows.
Who first handed you a key
which you thought was a knife, to stab you.
It wasn't a shadow. It was your foreshadow.
At night, see the brushstrokes your dreams, clearly,
but fall not into sleep with your eyes closed.
Let the dreams burn before you, like blue lanterns
on your origin, the altar.
Worship your life,
as do the butterflies the scent of a flower.
Bring yourself, entirely,
to the knowledge of your own colors.
Bow before the rainbow & yourself.
Now paint your life.

Which is another way to say,
Fall in love with yourself
until there is nothing else to love, just you.
My mother,
whenever she leaves the world for Syma,
sings this in her bedroom:

Fall in love with the love in you. Fall.
But how do I fall?   How?

Syma is the name of the village where I was born and raised and where I go fishing with my mother, who catered to the family in the absence of a father. After the announcement of the book as the Sillerman prize winner, I realized it is word, too, for the kingfisher. When I was a young boy I had a close affinity with kingfishers, seeing them in various colors and sizes on withered branches of mangrove trees stretched out over the river, but I never imagined I would be writing about them without knowing they shared the name of my home village. It is a double miracle—also in Syma, Sasha, my daughter, was conceived.

"Emerging," "Acts of a Green House," and "Maud, or Letter to the White
    Egrets" were inspired by Gwendolyn Brooks's poem "Maud Martha" and
    Cheswayo Mphanza's poem "When the World Ends, It Will Begin in
    New York, Letter to Maud Martha." I have included slight variations of
    the lines "Chicago is a decent place to fall in love" and "what she wanted
    was to donate to the world a good Maud Martha."
"Let There Be Lamplight" was inspired by Natasha Trethewey's poem
    "Reach."
"Altar" was inspired by Derek Walcott's "Love After Love."

Grateful acknowledgment is given to the publications where these poems first appeared.

"And The I Is the Revolution," *Loch Raven Review*
"The Origin," *Loch Raven Review*
"My Father's Last Hope for Water," *Eunoia Review*
"Let There Be Lamplight," *Konya Shamsrumi Magazine*

*Eight New-Generation African
Poets: A Chapbook Box Set*
Edited by Kwame Dawes
and Chris Abani
(Akashic Books)

*New-Generation African Poets:
A Chapbook Box Set (Tatu)*
Edited by Kwame Dawes
and Chris Abani
(Akashic Books)

*New-Generation African Poets:
A Chapbook Box Set (Nne)*
Edited by Kwame Dawes
and Chris Abani
(Akashic Books)

*New-Generation African Poets:
A Chapbook Box Set (Tano)*
Edited by Kwame Dawes
and Chris Abani
(Akashic Books)

*New-Generation African Poets:
A Chapbook Box Set (Sita)*
Edited by Kwame Dawes
and Chris Abani
(Akashic Books)

*New-Generation African Poets:
A Chapbook Box Set (Saba)*
Edited by Kwame Dawes
and Chris Abani
(Akashic Books)

*New-Generation African Poets:
A Chapbook Box Set (Nane)*
Edited by Kwame Dawes
and Chris Abani
(Akashic Books)

To order or obtain more information on these or other University of
Nebraska Press titles, visit nebraskapress.unl.edu. For more information
about the African Poetry Book Series, visit africanpoetrybf.unl.edu.